Lilith:
The Legend of the First Woman
By Ada Langworthy Collier
This Edition Edited by Anthony Uyl

Candle in the Dark Publishing
Ingersoll, Ontario, Canada 2023

Lilith: The Legend of the First Woman
By Ada Langworthy Collier
This Edition Edited By Anthony Uyl

The reformatted text of An Imaginary Trio is all protected under Copyright ©2023 Candle in the Dark Publishing. The covers, background, layout and Candle in the Dark Publishing logo are Copyright ©2023 Candle in the Dark Publishing. This edition is published by Candle in the Dark Publishing a division of 2165467 Ontario Inc.

Unless written permission is given for any material, all use of this material to be reproduced, stored in a retrieval system, or transmitted in any form by any means, electronic, mechanical, photocopying, recording or otherwise is forbidden. All rights reserved.

Drop Cap and Table of Contents fonts are AnglicanText by Typographer Mediengestaltung and used under a Free For Commercial Use License (FFC).

ISBN: 978-1-77356-457-9

Contact Us Online:
Email: office@candleinthedarkpub.com
Editors' Twitter: @AnthonyUyl
For more information on Biblical Demonology and issues with the occult in modern evangelicalism, check out the editors' Substack Blog Reformed Demonology: reformeddemonology.substack.com

Table of Contents

Preface - 5
To Valeria - 9
Lilith - 11
    Book I - 11
    Book II - 19
    Book III - 27
    Book IV - 41
    Book V - 55

Preface

That Eve was Adam's second wife was a common Rabbinic speculation. Certain commentators on Genesis adopted this view, to account for the double account of the creation of woman, in the sacred text, first in Genesis i. 27, and second in Genesis xi. 18. And they say that Adam's first wife was named Lilith, but she was expelled from Eden, and after her expulsion Eve was created. Abraham Ecchelensis gives the following account of Lilith and her doings: "There are some who do not regard spectres as simple devils, but suppose them to be of a mixed nature—part demoniacal, part human, and to have had their origin from Lilith, Adam's first wife, by Eblis, prince of the devils. This fable has been transmitted to the Arabs, from Jewish sources, by some converts of Mohamet from Cabbalism and Rabbinism, who have transferred all the Jewish fooleries to the Arabs. They gave to Adam a wife formed of clay, along with Adam, and called her Lilith, resting on the Scripture: 'Male and female created He them.'"—Legends of the Patriarchs and Prophets.—Baring Gould.

Lilith or Lilis.—In the popular belief of the Hebrews, a female spectre in the shape of a finely dressed woman, who lies in wait for, and kills children. The old Rabbins turned Lilith into a wife of Adam, on whom he begat demons and who still has power to lie with men and kill children who are not protected by amulets with which the Jews of a yet later period supply themselves as a protection against her. Burton in his Anatomy of Melancholy tells us: "The Talmudists say that Adam had a wife called Lilis, before he married Eve, and of her he begat nothing but devils." A commentator on Skinner, quoted in the Encyclopædia Metropolitana, says that the English word Lullaby is derived from Lilla, abi (begone,

Lilith)! In the demonology of the Middle Ages, Lilis was a famous witch, and is introduced as such in the Walpurgis night scene in Goethe's "Faust."—Webster's Dictionary.

> Our word Lullaby is derived from two Arabic words which mean "Beware of Lilith!"
> —Anon.

> Lilith, the supposed wife of Adam, after she married Eblis, is said to have ruled over the city of Damascus.
> —Legends of the Patriarchs and Prophets.
> —Baring Gould.

From these few and meagre details of a fabled existence, which are all that the author has been able to collect from any source whatever, has sprung the following poem. The poet feels quite justified in dissenting from the statements made in the preceding extracts, and has not drawn Lilith as there represented—the bloodthirsty sovereign who ruled Damascus, the betrayer of men, the murderer of children. The Lilith of the poem is transferred to the more beautiful shadow-world. To that country which is the abode of poets themselves. And about her is wrapt the humanizing element still, and everywhere embodied in the sweetest word the human tongue can utter—lullaby. Some critics declare that true literary art inculcates a lofty lesson—has a high moral purpose. If poets and their work must fall under this rigorous rule, then alas "Lilith" will knock at the door of public opinion with a trembling hand indeed. If the poem have either moral aim or lesson of any kind (which observe, gentle critic, it is by no means asserted that it has), it is simply to show that the strongest intellectual powers contain no elements adverse to the highest and purest exercise of the affectional nature. That, in its true condition, the noblest, the most cultured intellect, and the loveliest, sublimest moral and emotional qualities, together weave the web that clothes the world's great soul with imperishable beauty. The possessor of highest intellectual capacity will be also capable of highest developments in the latter qualities. The woman of true intellect is the woman of truest affection. For the rest let Lilith speak, whose life dropped unrecorded from the earliest world. It is the poet's hope that the chords of the mother-heart universal will respond to the song of the childless one. That in the survival of that one word lullaby, may be revivified the pathetic figure of one whose home, whose hope, whose Eden passed to another. Whose name living in the terrors of superstitious peoples, now lingers in Earth's sweetest utterance. That Pagan Lilith, re-baptized in the pure waters of maternal love, shall breathe to heathen and Christian motherhood alike, that most sacred love of Earth still throbbing through its tender lullaby.

    A. L. C.

To Valeria

Broideries and ancient stuffs that some queen
    Wore; nor gems that warriors' hilts encrusted;
    Nor fresh from heroes' brows the laurels green;
   Nor bright sheaves by bards of eld entrusted
To earth's great granaries—I bring not these.
   Only thin, scattered blades from harvests gleaned
Erewhile I plucked, may happen thee to please.
   So poor indeed, those others had demeaned
Themselves to cull; or from their strong, firm hands
   Down dropped about their feet with careless laugh,
Too broken for home gathering, these strands,
   Or else more useless than the idle chaff.
But I have garnered them. Yet, lest they seem
   Unworthy, and so shame Love's offering,
Amid the loose-bound sheaf stray flowers gleam.
   And fairer seeming make the gift I bring,
Lilies blood-red, that lit the waving field,
   And now are knotted through the golden grain.
Thou wilt not scorn the tribute I now yield,
   Nor even deem the foolish flowers vain.
So take it, and if still too slight, too small
   It seem, think 'tis a bloom that grew anear,
In other Springtime, the old garden wall.
   (That pale blue flower you will remember, dear.
The heedless world, unseeing, passed it by,
   And left it to the bee and you.) Then say,
"Because the hands that tended it are nigh
   No more, and little feet are gone away
That round it trampled down the beaded grass,
   Sweeter to me it is than musky spray

Of Southland; and dearer than days that pass
    In other summer-tides." This simple song
Read so, dear heart; Nay, rather white-souled one,
    Think 'tis an olden echo, wandered long
From a low bed where 'neath the westering sun
    You sang. And if your lone heart ever said
"Lo, she is gone, and cannot more be mine,"
    Say now, "She is not changed—she is not wed,—
She never left her cradle bed. Still shine
    The pillows with the print of her wee head."
So, mother-heart, this song, where through still rings
    The strain you sang above my baby bed,
I bring. An idle gift mayhap, that clings
    About old days forgotten long, and dead.
This loitering tale, Valeria, take.
    Perchance 'tis sad, and hath not any mirth,
Yet love thou it, for the weak singer's sake,
    And hold it dear, though yet is little worth,
This tale of Elder-world: of earth's first prime,
    Of years that in their grave so long have lain,
To-day's dull ear, through poets' tuneful rhyme
    No echo hears, nor mocking friar's strain.

July 17, 1884.

LILITH

BOOK I

Pure as an angel's dream shone Paradise.
Blue mountains hemmed it round; and airy sighs
Of rippling waters haunted it. Dim glades,
And wayward paths o'erflecked with shimmering shades,
And tangled dells, and wilding pleasances,
Hung moist with odors strange from scented trees.
Sweet sounds o'erbrimmed the place; and rare perfumes,
Faint as far sunshine, fell 'mong verdant glooms.
In that fair land, all hues, all leafage green
Wrapt flawless days in endless summer-sheen.
Bright eyes, the violet waking, lifted up
Where bent the lily her deep, fragrant cup;
And folded buds, 'gainst many a leafy spray—
The wild-woods' voiceless nuns—knelt down to pray.
There roses, deep in greenest mosses swathed,
Kept happy tryst with tropic blooms, sun-bathed.
No sounds of sadness surged through listening trees:
The waters babbled low; the errant bees
Made answer, murmurous; nor paled the hue
The jonquils wore; nor chill the wild breath grew
Of daisies clustered white in dewy croft;
Nor fell the tasseled plumes as satin soft
Upon the broad-leaved corn. Sweet all the day
O'erflowed with music every woodland way;
And sweet the jargonings of nested bird,
When light the listless wind the forest stirred.
Straight as the shaft that 'gainst the morning sun
The slender palm uprears, the Fairest one—

The first of womankind—sweet Lilith—stood,
A gracious shape that glorified the wood.
About her rounded shoulders warm and bare,
Like netted sunshine fell her lustrous hair;
The rosy flush of young pomegranate bells
Dawned on her cheeks; and blue as in lone dells
Sleep the Forget-me-nots, her eyes. With bent
Brows, sullen-creased, swart Adam gazed intent
Upon a leopard, crouched low in its place
Beneath his feet. Not once in Lilith's face
He looked, nor sought her wistful, downcast eyes
With shifting shadows dusk, and strange surprise.
"O, Love," she said, "no more let us contend!
So sweet is life, anger, methinks, should end.
In this, our garden bright, why dost thou claim
Ever the highest place, the noblest name?
Freely to both our Lord gave self-same sway
O'er living things. Love, thou art gone astray!
Twin-born, of equal stature, kindred soul
Are we; like dowed with strength. Yon stars that roll
Their course above, down-looking on my face,
See yours as fair; in neither aught that's base.
Thy wife, not handmaid I, yet thou dost say,
'I first in Eden rule.' Thou, then, hast sway.
Must I, my Adam, mutely follow thee?
Run at thy bidding, crouch beside thy knee?
Lift up (when thou dost bid me) timid eyes?
Not so will Lilith dwell in Paradise."
"Mine own," Adam made answer soft, "'twere best
Thou didst forget such ills in noontide rest.
Content I wake, the keeper of the place.
Of equal stature? Yea! Of self-same grace?
Nay, Love; recall those lately vanished eves,
When we together plucked the plantain leaves;
Yon leopard lowly stretched at my command
Its lazy length beneath my soothing hand.
At thee she snarled, disdaining half, to sheathe
'Neath thy soft pleading eyes her milk-white teeth.
Oft, Love, in other times, in sheltered nook,

We scattered pearly millet by the brook.
Lo thine lay barren in the sand. Quick mine
Upspringing sifts o'er pale blooms odors fine:
Hateful thy chidings grow; each breeze doth bring
Ever thy plaints—thy fretful murmuring.
These many days I weary of thy sighs;
Know, Lilith, I alone rule Paradise."
Thereat he rose, and quick at every stride
The fawning leopard gambolled at his side.
So fell the first dark shadow of Earth's strife.
With coming evil all the winds were rife.
Lone lay the land with sense of dull loss paled.
The days grew sick at heart; the sunshine failed;
And falling waters breathed in silvery moan
A hidden ail to starlit dells alone—
As sometimes you have seen, 'neath household eaves,
'Mong scents of Springtime, in the budded leaves,
The swallows circling blithe, with slant brown wing,
Home-flying fleet, with tender chattering,
And all the place o'errun with nested love—
So have you come, when leaves hung crisp above
The silent door. Yet not again, I ween,
Those shining wings, cleaving the air, have seen
Nor heard the gladsome swallows twittering there—
Only the empty nests, low-hung and bare,
Spake of the scattered brood.—So lonely were
To Lilith grown her once loved haunts. Nor fair
The starlit nights, slow-dropping fragrant dew,
Nor the dim groves when dawn came shifting through.
Far 'mong the hills the wood-doves' moan she heard,
Or in some nearer copse, a startled bird;
Or the white moonshine 'mong green boughs o'erhead
Wrought her full heart to tears. "Sweet peace," she said,
"Alas—lies slain!"
    With musing worn, she brake
At last her silence, and to Adam spake:
"Beyond these walls I know not what may be—
Islands low-fringed, or bare; or tranquil sea,
Spaces unpeopled, wastes of burning sands,

Green-wooded belts, enclasping summer lands,
Or realms of dusky pines, or wolds of snow,
Or jagged ice-peaks wrapt in purple glow,
Or shadowy oceans lapped in fadeless sheen—
Yet there were Paradise, were Lilith queen.
To dally with my lord I was not meant;
To soothe his idle whims, above him bent,
Warm in my milk-white arms, lull his repose,
Nor deep in subtle kisses drown his woes.
Wherefore, since here no more dwells love, I fly
To seek my home in other lands. For why
Should Lilith wait since Adam's empty state
More dear he holds than Lilith desolate?"
But answer soft made Adam at the word,
For faint his dying love, yet coldly stirred
Its ashen cerements: "Nay, love, our home
Within these garden walls lies safe. Wouldst roam
Without? Sweet peace, by loss, wilt thou restore
One little loss, or miss it evermore?"
"In goodly Eden, Adam, safely bide,
But I, for peace, nor love, nor life," she cried,
"Submit to thee. Unto our Lord I own
Allegiance true; my homage his alone.
Oft have I watched the mists athwart yon peaks,
Pursuing oft past coves and winding creeks,
Have thought to touch their shining veil outspread,
In happy days ere Love, alas, was dead;
So now, farewell! Ere the new day shall break
Adown their gleaming track, my way I take."
She turned; but ere the gate that looked without
She reached, one fleeting moment paused in doubt
Upon a river's brink. In one swift glance
All coming time she saw. A weird romance
Wherein she traced great peoples yet unborn,
New springing cycles, strange lands cleft with tarn
Or pleasant vale, and green plains stretching far,
And quiet bays, and many a shingly bar,
And troubled seas, with bitter perils past,
And elfin shapes that jeering flitted fast

With scornful faces, leering lips that smiled,
Or bursts of laughter through that vision wild.
Uncertain, then, she stood, half loth to turn.
"Against yon deepening sky, how dimly burn
The stars, new-lit. Dear home, thou art so fair!"
She fondly sighed.
    Then sudden she was 'ware
The angel near her paused, whose watchful care
Guards Eden's peaceful bounds. Serene, his air
So tender-sweet, so pure the gentle face,
She scarce dared look upon its subtle grace.
Sad were his eyes; his words, rebuking, fell
Soft as the moonshine clear, in sleeping dell.
"My sister, go not hence, lest these gates bar
Lilith forever out. From peace afar,
Anger and pride shall lead through distant ways
Thy feet reluctant, in the evil days.
All is decreed. At yonder southern gate
Behold! waits even now my princely mate.
Thou can'st not tell which hath in our far land
The highest place. Nay; nor, indeed, whose hand
Hath grasped the noblest fame; nor yet divine
Whose brows enwound with honor, brightest shine.
In pleasant labor lurks no thought of pain;
The greatest loss oft brings the noblest gain;
The heart's warm pulse feels not one throb of strife,
And Love is holiest crown of human life.
Ere thou didst sleep, beyond the rim of night
I heard a voice that sang. The carol light,
Scarce earth-born seemed. So sweet the matchless strain,
Its cadence weird, lowly to breathe again,
Wrapt echo, listening, half forgot; and o'er
And o'er, as joyous birds unprisoned soar,
The free notes rose. And in the silence wide,
Across the seas, across the night, I cried:
O sinless soul, whose clear voice blithely rings
'Gainst the blue verge of stars! 'Tis Lilith sings
The happy song of love. O Love! the tint
Of light divine thou wearest. Thou hast no hint

Of storm or turmoil, or of Sin's rough ways,
Whose feet to heaven climb, through darkest maze.
Ah, Lilith, sure the love that basely weighs,
That stoops to count its gifts, and hoarding, says,
'Such and so many, these indeed are mine;
 I hold my treasure dear, nor covet thine;'
This is not love; 'tis Thrift in borrowed dress,
Deceiving thee. Love giveth free largess
With open hand, clean as the whitest day;
Yea, that it gave, forgetteth it straightway.
Beyond these walls dwells bliss that lives not here?
When thou hast bartered peace, outshining clear
And storm-tossed wide, art wildly driven hence,
The outer world gives thee no recompense.
Each shining sphere that trembles in blue space
Hath orbit true—its own familiar place.
Nor doth the planet pale that gems the night
Reel wanton down, the smallest star to smite.
No twining vine, tendril, or springing shoot
Ere taught thee so; for bud and leaf and root
Doth its best self lift upward into light,
Yet climbing still, scorns not the sacred right
hat shrines its fellow.
    "So pattering rains
The dark roots drink—and healthful juice slow drains
Deep 'neath the mould; and with their secret toil
Bear stainless, leaf and flow'r above the soil.
Noblest the soul that self hath most forgot;
Strongest the self which hath most humbly wrought;
Purest the soul that in full light serene,
Unquestioning, enwrapt, God's field doth glean.
I have seen worlds far hence; thy tender feet
Bleeding, will tread their stony ways. And sweet
Is love. And wedded love, grown cold and rude,
More bitter-seeming makes dull solitude.
Security is sweet; and light and warm
The young heart beats, close shut from every harm."
"Yet," Lilith answered slow, "in that still night
Ere He, the garden's Lord, passed from our sight,

Hast thou forgot his words? 'Lo this fair spot
Made for your pleasance; see ye mar it not,
Oh, twin-born pair! So richly dight with grace
Of soul and stature; unto whom the place
I give. Together rule. Bear equal sway
O'er all that live herein.' Hath Lilith sought
A solitary reign? Hath she in aught
Offended? Nay; 'tis Adam who doth break
The compact. Therefore, unhindered let me take
My way far hence. I shall not vex his soul
With fretful plaints, where unknown stars shall roll,
Far, far away," she sighed.
    "Yet ere these bounds
Thy feet pass, linger. Lilith, list glad sounds
That greet thine ear. Slow cycles will pass on
And in the time-to-be-bright years, grow wan;
Old planets fade, new stars shall dimly burn,
But not to Eden's peace shalt thou return.
Oft from thy yearning heart glad hope shall fail.
Thy fruit of life lift bloom all sere and pale.
Certain, small comfort bides, when joy is gone,
In Great or Less. Grim Sorrow waits to lead thee on.
Sorrow! Thou hast not seen her pallid face.
In thy most troubled dream she had no place"—
"Nay, I depart," she said, with lips grown chill.
"Fearless and free, exiled, but princess still."
"I may not hinder thee," the Angel sighed;
"No soul unwilling here may ever bide."
Slow swung the verdant gates neath saddest eyes.
Lilith forever lost fair Paradise.

Book II

Soft stealing through the shade, and skirting swift
The walls of Paradise, through night's dark rift
Lilith fled far; nor stopped lest deadly snare
Or peril by the wayside lurked.
    The air
Grew chill. Loud beat her heart, as through the wind
Echoed, unseen, pursuing feet, behind.
Adown the pathway of the mist she passed,
And reached a weird, strange land at last.
When morning flecked the dappled sky with red,
And odors sweet from waking flowers were shed,
Lilith beheld a plain, outstretching wide,
With distant mountains seamed.
    Afar, a silvery tide
The blue shore kissed. And in that tropic glow
Dim islands shone, palm-fringed, and low.
In nearer space, like scarlet arrows flew
Strange birds, or 'mong the reedy fens, or through
Tall trees, of unknown leafage, glancing, went.
Now Lilith seaward passed, and stooping, bent
Her hollowed hand above the wave, and quaffed;
For she was spent with wanderings wide. Loud laughed
She then, beholding on that silent shore
Rare shells, that still faint in their pink lips bore
Wild ocean-songs; and precious stones, that bright
That dim sea's marge, deep in the land of night
Thick strewed.
    Then glad, she lifted shining eyes,
Loud crying there, "O Lilith, now arise,
Great queen-triumphant! See how wildly fair
Before me lies my realm! And from its air

Soft, sensuous, new life as ruddy wine,
My spirit drinks. Nor beauty so divine
Hath Eden's self. Look, where upon the sands
The garish mosses spread with dainty hands,
Like goblin network fine, each fairy frond.
And dusky trees shut in broad fields beyond,
And hang long trembling garlands, age-grown-gray,
From topmost boughs adown, athwart the day;
And sweet amid these wilds, bright dewy bells
Ring summer chimes. And soft in fragrant dells,
'Mong tender leaves, great spikes of scarlet flaunt
About the pools—the errant wild bees' haunt—
And thick with bramble-blooms pink petals starred,
And dew-stained buds of blue, the velvet sward.
Scarce ripple stirred the sea; and inland wend
Far bays and sedgy ponds; and rolling rivers bend.
A land of leaf and fruitage in the glow
Of palest glamours steeped. And far and low
Great purple isles; and further still a rim
Of sunset-tinted hills, that softly dim
Shine 'gainst the day. "O world, new found," she said,
"With treasures heaped and odors rare, 'mong flowers shed,
For whose dear sake I came o'er flinty ways,
And paths with danger fraught; 'mong brambly sprays,
With bleeding feet, and shoulders thorn-pierced deep.
But perils past, fade fast. And I will weep
My Eden lost no more." And sweet and low
As one who dreams, she said, "For now I know
These mountain heights, these level plains, are mine."
She ceased, and inland quickly turned. "Fair shine
Strange fruits thick-set, or blossoms lightly tossed
Low at my feet." Therewith, a dusk globe, crossed
With golden bands, from bent boughs, stripped she. Through
The gleaming sphere its nectrous juices drew,
And thirsting cried—as one grown drunken: "Mine
These fruits unknown, in thorny combs that shine,
Or gray-green spikes that glow, dull on the sands.
Fain would I pluck, out-reaching eager hands,
Save that a marvel grows of ruddier rind

Out-flinging fruity breath upon the wind,
Beneath harsh spines half-hid. Nor drains
My wilful spouse such nectars fine. Nor gains
His patient care the fruitage rare, these plains
That heaps unheeded. Nay, nor bearded grains
Golding this goodly land, where Lilith reigns."
So passed the glad years on, and o'er her home—
Its woods and mountains, its clear streams—to roam,
She loved. The inmost throb of Nature's heart
She felt amid the grass. Each daintiest part
Of Nature's work she knew; each gain, each loss.
And reverent watched on high the starry cross
Gleaming, mute symbol in that southern dome
Of One—the Promised One—of days to come.
The rifted sea-shell on the shingly beach
She scanned, pitying each inmate gone. Each
Named. 'Mong beetling crags, the sea-bird's home,
Light-footed, went. Or, idly, in the foam
Under the cocoa-palms, her fingers dipped,
Much marveling to see where featly slipped
Beneath the waves scaled creatures, crimson-dyed
Or luminous: Barred-yellow, purple pied,
Rose-tinted, opaline, or dight with stain,
Rich as the rainbow streaks, when through the rain
The Sun's kiss falls. Much wondered she when bright
By sedgy pools, flamingoes stalked. And light
The startled ostrich bent his headlong flight
O'er desert bare. And on the woody height
Trooped zebras, velvet-brown. The date's green crest
Beneath, the peaceful camels lay at rest.
And slender-straight camelopards the boughs
Down-drew, the lush-green leaves thereon to browse.
Or oft 'mong oozy bogs, or through the fens,
Fearless she went, when low, 'mong reedy dens
The water-courses by, huge creatures slept,
Or in the jungles spotted panthers crept,
And in the thickets deadly serpents wound
Like blossomed wreaths, their coils upon the ground.
All forms of life she saw; with tenderest care

Uplifting humblest sprays, or blooms most rare.
Pierced the deep heart of Nature's subtlest lore,
Touched highest knowledge, probed the inmost core
Of hidden things. She tracked each circling world
And the wide sweep of billows lightly curled.
Each page the Master writ she read, close furled
In lotus blooms, or, 'mong the storm-clouds whirled;
Or traced, star-lettered, on the flaming scroll
The night unwinds toward the southern pole.
And sometimes wiling idle days, she wove
In quaint device, gems from her treasure-trove,
Rare garlanded, or set in flashing zone
Soft emerald, sapphire pale, and many a stone
Out-gleaming amethyst. Her yellow hair
Among, the glinting diamonds shone. And there
The sultry topaz burned. And laughing, twined
She round her bare white throat red rubies shrined
In pearls.
  Or she among the haunts would rove
That sheltered island birds; or in the grove,
Or 'mong the rocky cliffs, where dainty nests
They fashioned swift. She scaled the seaward crests,
And on the sands piled turtle eggs, when all
About hoarse-shrieked the water-fowl, or call
Of plovers fell among the tangled glens,
Or lonely bitterns' boom came o'er the fens.
So traversed she her realm, when mangoes green
Baobabs by, showed freshest hues; and sheen
Of silver touched acacias slight; and lone
The solitary aloes, dreamed. The moan
Of that far sea against the shore brake soft.
And through that blossom-burdened land as oft
She roamed and far, sweet sped the passing days.
Till one dawned fairest, in whose noon-tide haze
Sweet slumbering she lay; and dreamed-steeped still,
Half conscious, caught the tinkle of a rill
In far-off Paradise. More silver clear
Across her thoughts, as once she loved to hear,
Rippled the waters, low against the stones

Where poised gemmed dragon-flies; and sudden moans
Shook 'mong blue flags. Waked, vague unrest
And tender yearning rose within her breast,
And longing love, that she ne'er more might still.
When late upon her parting day smiled chill,
Pensive she gazed upon the darkling land,
With lingering feet o'er-passed the shining strand,
And silent sat on an o'erhanging ledge,
The sea o'erlooking. Far the horizon's edge
Athwart her gaze a rim of blue hills cleft,
Whereat she sighed. "So rose, ere I them left,
So smiled, the dim hills round my Eden home.
But I—wherefore recall, when far I roam,
Dreams vanished—gone? And now since long time dead
Is that fair past, I fain would lay it low
Where soft about it memories sweet may blow
As summer winds the fallen leaves among."
Then passed her tender thoughts, and loud and glad
 As our morn wakens, strong that yesternight slept sad,
She sang. The song triumphant upward swelled,
Unsorrowed by soft dreams or thoughts of eld—
As fresh the full, free, mellow notes did rise
As the blithe skylark's strain, anear the skies:

    High, high, bold Eagle, soar;
I watch thy flight, above thy craggèd rock.
    Below thee, torrents roar,
Down-bursting wild with angry shock
    Upon the vales. O proud bird, free,
    My spirit, mounting, follows thee,
    Still follows thee, still follows thee.

    O Sea—O Sea so wide!
Far roll thy waves ere yet they find thy shore.
    I hear thy sullen tide
Break 'neath the beetling cliffs with muffled roar.
    Afar, afar, O moaning Sea,
    My roving soul still follows thee,
    Still follows thee, still follows thee.

O Whirlwind black—O strong!
Thy scorching breath fierce burns the crouching land
    And thou dost sweep along
The raveled clouds. O Whirlwind, see—
    My spirit rising, follows thee,
    Still follows thee, still follows thee.

    Nay, nay! My dauntless soul,
Still higher than thy wing, O Eagle, soars,
    And wider still than roll
Thy waves, and further than thy shores,
    My spirit flees—O Sea—O Sea
    No more it follows, follows thee.

    Whirlwind, more strong than thou
My soul, that fearless leaps to thine embrace
    And thy stern, wrinkled brow
Doth tender touch and soothingly,
    And vassal art thou still to me,
    That no more, Whirlwind, follows thee.

Swift changed her mood, and darkened in her face.
As sometimes in an open, sunny place
The sudden dusks o'er crinkling waters run,
So fell her thoughts to music. And as one
That grieves, she sang. That lay—soft, weirdly clear,
The babbling waves made murmurous pause to hear:

Fair land (she sang), O sun-steeped realm of mine,
The Sun, thy lover, hath his farewell kiss.
    I only pine
    While dim stars shine.

Strong is thy Day-god! yet his parting kiss
Falls soft upon thy faltering lips. O land,
    Thou hast a bliss
    I ever miss.

Fast comes the night, and warm, for thy dear sake,
The shadows curtain dusk, thy lonely rest.
    I only wake

>   My plaint to make.

Fair land, my lover cold, doth careless take
From my shut lips his flight. Here leaves me lone
>   My moan to make,
>   My heart to break.

She ceased. But still the song did float and fade,
As failing sunshine soft, in woodland glade.
And Lilith, listening, heard—so wild, so shrill,
Yet dream-like, far, again that tinkling rill
In Paradise. And o'er her spirit swept
A sadness bitter-sweet, as 'neath the green palms crept
The wind, low-sighing, faint. As from lone nest
A bird torn pinion lifts, striving to soar
To shelter safe, so, Edenward once more
Turned Lilith's drooping thoughts.
>   Uprose she then,
And brooding, homeward slowly went again.

Book III

Wide through her realm she walked, and glad or lorn
She mused. So, loitering, it chanced one morn
When lone she sat upon a mountain height,
One sudden stood anear, whose dark eyes bright
Upon her shone. Pallid his face, and red
His smileless lips. "Who art thou?" Lilith said,
And faint a hidden pain her hot heart stirred,
When low, and rarely sweet, his voice she heard.
She looked, half-pleased—and half in strange surprise
Shrank 'neath the gaze of those wild, starry eyes.
"Oh, dame," the stranger said, "where waters leap
Bright glancing down, I rested oft, where steep
Thy Eden o'er, bare-browed, a peak uprose.
Naught craving bloom or fruitage—nay, nor those
Frail joys Adam holds dear. One only boon
I sought of all his heritage. Fair 'neath the moon
I saw thee stand; and all about thy feet
The night her perfume spilled, soft incense meet.
Then low I sighed, when grew thy beauty on my sight,
'Some comfort yet remains, if that I might
From Adam pluck this perfect flower. Some morn—
If I (some dreamed-of morn, perchance slow-born)
This flawless bloom, white, fragrant, lustrous, pure
For ever on my breast might hold secure.'
Yea, for thy love, through darkling realms of night
I followed thee, sharing thy fearful flight
Unseen. Lo, when thy timid heart, behind
Heard echoing phantom feet upon the wind,
'Twas I, pursuing o'er the day's last brink;
Wherefore, I now am here. O Lilith, think

How over-much I love thee, and how sweet
Were life with thee! O weary naked feet,
With me each onward path wilt thou not tread?
Or, if thou endest here thy quest," he said,
"Let me too bide with thee."
    Made answer low
Lilith thereto: "Meseems not long ago
One stood at Eden's gate like thee. But thy face
Is darker, red thy lips. Of kingly race
I know thee. Say, whence comest thou, O prince?"
"Nay, then," he sighed, "an outcast I, long since
From Heaven thrust out; yet now, the curse is past,
Nor mourn I Heaven lost, if at the last
Thy love I win. Yea, where thou art, I know
Is Heaven. And bliss, in sooth" (oh, soft and low,
He said), "lives ever in thy smile."
    His speech
Thus ended. And toward the sandy beach
He passed. Though long her eyes the stranger sought
Where curved the distant shore, she saw him not.

Soft through the trees the mottled shadows dropped
When Lilith in her pleasance sat. Half-propped
'Gainst mossy trunk her slender length. Her hair
In sunny web, enmeshed her elbows bare.
Slowly the breeze swayed the mimosas slight
As Eblis pushed aside the bent boughs light.
"O dame," he said, "it seemeth surely meet
Earth's richest gifts to lay at Lilith's feet;
Therefore I said 'unto the fairest one,
Things loveliest beneath the shining sun
I bring.' Since of all crafts in this young earth
I am true master, unto her whose worth
So much deserves, I bear this marble sphere,
Whose hollowed husk, well polished, gleaming clear,
Hides rarest fruit." Therewith the globe he showed,
The half whereof smooth-sparkling was: Half glowed
With carven work; embossed with pale leaves light,
And delicately sculptured birds in flight,
And clustered flowers frail. Lilith drew near

With beaming eyes, and laid the graven sphere
Against her smiling lips; o'ertraced the vine
That circled it with fingers slim. "Mine, mine
Is it, O prince?" she cried. "I know not why
Its beauty doth recall the winds' long sigh
That surged among the palms. Methinks is dead
Some summer-tide, that in its own sweet stead
Hath left upon the stone its imaging."
Eblis replied: "On earth, is anything
More fair? If such thou knowest, Lilith, speak.
That I, for thee, surely would straightway seek.
Say, if indeed thou findest anywhere,
On land or sea, created things so rare?"
And Lilith answered, "On this earth so round,
Naught else so lovely anywhere I found.
So shames it meaner work—so had I said—
But see yon nodding palm that droops its head
Low sighing o'er the wave. Bring me a bough
So feathery-fine. Turn thy white sphere! Now
On its cold, fair surface, Eblis, canst thou
Such branches carve, or tender fronds, that we
Bright waving on the cocoa, these may see?"
And Eblis wrought till grew upon the stone
Such airy boughs as on the cocoa shone.
Then Lilith cried: "Skilled craftsman, proven thou!
Didst thou, then, make my cocoa-tree? Thy bough
Pale graven give the grace of its green crown
When through it night winds gently slip adown.
No charm of color, nor of change, nor glow
Of blue noon sky, thy carven work doth show;
Let dusk bees visit it—or sip the breath
From thy chill marble buds." Then, Lilith saith,
"Eblis hath wroughten noblest on this earth."
He answered quick, "Poor bauble, little worth
To Lilith! Ope thy slighted husk, reveal
The miracle thy rough rind doth conceal!"
He touched a hidden spring, and wide apart
The riven sphere showed its white hollow heart,
And in the midst a gem; the which he laid

Within her hand. "Behold," he said, "I made
Most fair for thee this lustrous blood-red sard,
And deftly traced its gleaming surface hard
With carvings thick of bright acacias slim,
Pomegranates lush and river-reeds. Its rim
A spray of leaves enchased, white as with rime
Night fallen. 'Slow drags the lagging time,'
I said, 'till one day shines upon the breast
Of her, whose perfect beauty worthiest
It decks, this gem.' The token, Lilith, take;
If lovelier there be, for Eblis' sake
Keep silent; yet with me, oh Lilith, go
Awhile from thine own land. Then shall I know
The gem finds favor in thine eyes."
    Then she
Turned from her pleasance and all silently
Passed to the sea, across the yellow strand
That, glimmering, ringed her shadowy land.
"Oh cool," he said, "the lucent waves that fret
The barren shore, and curl their scattered spray wet
'Gainst thy hand. Come! my longing pinnace waits
To bear thee far. Her slender keel now grates
Upon the beach; and swift her shapely prow
Will skim the deep, as swallows' fleet wing. Thou
Seest! comely and strong it is. For thee
Its golden sails, its purple canopy.
With skin of spotted pard, I cushioned it.
Ere the fresh breeze doth die, light let us flit
Across the sea. No craft so proud, so staunch,
Goes glancing through the foam. I safely launch
Her now, and speed to fairy isles. Come thou
With me." And glad she crossed the burnished prow;
And 'mong the thick furred rugs sat down. "Oh craft,
Fair fashioned, lightly built, speed far," she laughed;
"To other lands bear Lilith safe."
    As sailed
They idly on, her slender hand she trailed
Among the waves, and sudden cried, "Indeed,
A craft stauncher than thine floats by. What need

Hath it of helm, or prow, or silken sail,
Sure harbor finding when the ocean gale
Fast drives it onward?" A nut she drew, round,
Rough, coarse-husked, forth from the wave. "Lo, I found,"
She said, "this boat well built. The cocoa-tree
Cast it amid the foam. Its pilot free,
The summer wind; its port, the misty shore
Of ocean isles. It fades from sight. 'No more,'
We say, 'it sails the wild uncertain main,'
But when the drifting days are gone, again
We turn our prow, and reach the barren isles
Where, stranded as we went, the nut. Now smiles
Above; a bending tree. Aloud we cry,
'A miracle is wrought!' We draw anigh.
Behold, the cocoa, towering, doth spring
Forth from the brown nut's heart. About it cling
Sweet odors faint; and far stars trembling peep.
When through its bowers cool the breezes creep.
Strong, indeed, thy boat, well builded! I wis
There be yet other craft as firm, Eblis,
That o'er these trackless waters boldly glide.
Brave Nautilus afar, doth fearless ride,
With sails of gossamer. So, too, doth spread,
To summer airs, his silken gleaming thread,
The water-spider fleet, free sailor true
That in the sunshine floats, beneath the blue,
Glad skies. And through the deep, all sparkling, slip
A thousand insect-swarms, that, rippling, dip
Amid the merry waves. Bright voyagers
That roam the sultry seas! Look, the wind stirs
Our creaking sails! Thy pinnace flying o'er
The ocean's swell, fast leaves the fading shore;
Yet faster still the Nautilus sails by,
And darts the spider quick. And swifter fly
The insect-fleets among the foam; yet think
Not when among the billows wild doth sink
Thy bounding boat, I fear. Nor would I slight
Thy skill, that made it strong, and swift, and light,
And trimmed it gayly, for my sake."

Now near
A jutting shore Prince Eblis drew, where sheer
The brown rocks rose. And just beyond, a slim
Beach of white sand curved to the ocean's brim.
Thereto he came, and high upon the strand
Drew the boat's keel. "Welcome, fair queen, to land
That Eblis rules," he said. "I fain would show
Thee what thou hast not seen in the warm glow
Of thy glad home. This blighted shore of mine
No verdure hath, nor bloom, nor fruits that shine
'Mong drooping boughs. Far inland gloom lone peaks
O'er blackened meads; or from their bare cones leaps
Gaunt, crackling flame; or crawl like ashen veins
The smouldering fires across the stricken plains.
Deep in these yawning caves black shadows lie
That shall be lifted never more. Come, I
Enter! Know thou what treasure by the sea
I gathered other time." Therewith showed he
Hid 'mong the high heaped rocks a dusky grot
Where never sunshine fell. A dismal spot
Where dank the sea-weeds coiled and cold the air
Swept through. And stooping, Eblis downward rolled
Before her webs of woven stuff, in fold
Of purple sheen, enwrought with flecks of gold.
Great wefts of scarlet and of blue, thick strewn
With pearls, or cleft with discs of jacinth stone;
And drifts of silky woof and samite white,
And warps of Orient hues. Eblis light
Wound round her neck a scarf of amber. Wide
Its smooth folds sweeping flowed; and proud he cried,
"Among these hills, in the still loom of night,
I wrought for Lilith's pleasing, all. And bright
Have spun these webs, in blended morning hues
And noontide shades and trail of silver dews—
Hereon have set fair traceries of cloud-shine
And tints of the far vales. The textures fine
Glow with sweet thoughts of thee. And otherwhere
Hast thou such fabrics seen, or colors rare
As these?" Dawned in her eyes a swift delight,

And low she cried, "Oh, wondrous is the sight,
And much it pleaseth me. But yet," she said,
"Beside my knee one morn, its hooded head
A Hagè reared. Its gliding shape so near
To subtler music moved, than my dull ear
Could catch. Its velvet skin I gently strake,
Watching the light that o'er its heaped coils brake
In glittering waves. Within its small, wise glance,
Flame silent slept, or quick in baleful dance
Before my startled gaze quivering did wake.
Fair is thy woof, soft woven, yet the snake
Out-dazzles it. The beetle that doth boom
Its dull life out among the tangled gloom,
Lift his wide wing above thy weft, or trail
His splendor there, and thy poor web will pale;
Yea, the red wayside lily that doth snare
The girdled bee, is softer still, more fair
Than finest woven cloth." But tenderly
She smoothed the gleaming folds. "Much pleaseth me,
Natlhess," she said, "such loveliness." Then brought
He tapestries of fleeces fine, well wrought
In colors soft as woodland mosses' tinge,
Or glow of autumn blooms: Heavy with fringe
Of downward sweeping gold; arras, where through
Showed mottled stripes, or arabesques of blue,
Broad zones of red, and tender grays, and hue
Of dropping leaves. "Lilith," he said, "when rolled
The storm-tossed billows round these caves, behold
I spun these daintily. 'Twere hard to find
Such twisted weft or woven strand." "Oh, kind,"
She said, "is Eblis, unto whom I fain
Would give due thanks. His gorgeous train
But yesterday I saw the peacock spread;
Bright in the sun gleamed his small crested head;
His haughty neck wrinkled to green and blue,
And since I needs must truly speak, I knew
Not color rich as his: and I have seen
The curious nest among the branches green,
The busy weaver-bird plaits of thick leaves,

And in and out its pliant meshes weaves;
And since thou sayest 'twere hard to match thy fine,
Strong, woven fabrics, watch the weaver twine
His cunning wefts. Though still," she said, "think not
I scorn thy gifts, Prince Eblis; for I wot
Their worth is greater than my tongue can say."
 Then Eblis deeper in the cave led her a little way,
And showed a stately screen of such fine art
One almost felt the breeze that seemed to part
The pictured boughs. And o'er the stirless lake
Dreamed the swift, wimpling waters sudden brake
Among the willows on its brink—and flowers
Of scarlet, shining-clean from summer showers;
And Eblis said, "Cold praise a friend should spare
This picture true. Certain naught else will dare
Vie with such beauty."
    Archly Lilith took
The rose from her bright hair, and lightly shook
The dewdrop from its heart. "I loving, touch,"
She said, "these petals smooth. O, Eblis, such
Give to thy painted blooms; give its cool sheen
Of morningtide, the mossy, lush leaves green
That fold it round. Give its faint, fragrant breath,
When with the fickle breeze it dallieth.
Nay, fairer still my rose than gilded screen,
Though it be limned with perfect art, I ween."
Thereat smiled Eblis bitterly. "I bring
One parting gift," he said, "a dainty thing;
Perchance in other time it will recall
One who strove long and patiently through all
These days to win thy praise." An oval plane
Of crystal gave he her; of fleck or stain
Clear-gleaming. Of ivory carven fine
The frame. And when she looked, "Divine,"
He laughed, "the beauty it enshrines. Canst claim
Aught else is fairer?" And Lilith again
Gazed in the glass, her face beholding there,
Her pink flushed cheeks, her yellow streaming hair.
Quick came her breath. "O prince," she slowly said,

"Fair is the stranger. Bid those lips so red
Speak once to Lilith. For methinks the voice
Of such in music flowed. Let me rejoice
Therein." "O glorious counterfeit!" cried
He. "Lovelier is not on this earth wide!
Behold, sweet Lilith, 'tis thine own pure face
That lends my happy mirror perfect grace
It else had not. Bid thou thine image speak!
No other happiness I elsewhere seek,
If the soft tale she whispers be of me."
And Lilith answered gravely, "I know thee,
Eblis. Master indeed of all crafts thou—
Red Sard, and marble sphere, and agile prow
Of pinnace light well wroughten were by thee
And decked full fair. And, beauteous to see,
Fine woven weft and web, and the tall screen
O'errun with painted bloom, crystal, with gleam
Of Lilith's face—thou madest these. Mayhap
Beetle and asp likewise didst tint—didst wrap
The green about my rose, and richly fringe
My cocoa-tree, or peacock's train didst tinge
With dazzling hues. Methought thou wert a prince,
But now Lilith should humbly kneel, since
Thou art far higher than she deemed, if thou
Madest these wondrous things." And lowly now
As she would kneel, she drew anigh. But he
Cried, shrinking, "Nay, I made them not." And she
Low questioned, "Eblis, tell me who then, did make
Them all. Who set the creeping hooded snake
And stealthy pard within the thorny brake,
And spread the sea, and wreathed the waterfall
With foam? Who reared the hoar hills, towering tall
Above the lands?" With eyes wild flashing, low
He groaned: "O Lilith, ask me not. My foe
He was—he is. Trembles with wrath my frame
If I but faintly breathe his awful name."
Lilith replied, "Meseemeth, master true
Of every craft is He."
      Forth the two

From that drear cavern passed. Ere the water's brim
They gained, he plucked the wilding reeds, that slim
Stood by a brook. "My pipe I make, one strain
Harmonious to wake. Nor yet again
Shalt thou such fresh notes hear. Music like mine
Methinks thou hast not known in any time."
He laid his pipe unto his lips, and blew
A blast, wild, piercing, sweet. The far hills through
It rung. And softer fell, yet wild and clear.
It ceased. With drooping eyes, "Once I did hear
A song as wildly clear, as sad," she said,
"In mine own realm." And as she spoke, dark dread
The sky grew with a coming storm. "Oh, haste,"
He cried; "seek refuge ere this dreary waste
Reeks with the rain!" And fast they sped
Back to his ocean-cave. There safe, o'erhead
They watched the piling clouds. With angry roar
The baffled billows broke upon the rocks. O'er
Them rushed the shrieking storm. Wild through the grot
Wandered the prisoned wind, a troubled ghost that sought
Repose. Or low did moan, and trembling, wail,
Like some sore-hearted thing that hideth, pale,
And dare not front the day; and wilder still,
In chords melodious, swelled or sank, until
She sighed, "Oh, this weird harp among the caves,
Strange players hath! For loud as one that raves,
It rises. Now more sweetly fade away
Its mellow notes than thy thin pipes." "One day,"
He said, "mayhap my strain may please, when wind
Doth not outpipe my slighted reeds. Unkind
Thou art." "The storm is past; to mine own land
I would return," she said. And Eblis o'er the strand
Led her. And homeward silent turned his prow
That swiftly through the swirling waves did plow.
But when they parted, Eblis mused, "I know
No gift soever winneth her, rich though
It be and seemly. Into this pure soul,
Through fear of ill, I enter; or by goal
Of future gain before it set."

So came
He to her pleasance yet again. A flame
Leaped high above a brazier that he bore,
Its sweet, white, scented wood quick lapping o'er.
With darkened face Eblis above her hung.
"This hath, than my poor pipe, a keener tongue,"
Smileless and stern, he said. "Oh, dame,
List how the wild, crisp, crackling ruby flame
Eats through the tender boughs. A trusty knave
It is, that serves me well, and loud doth rave
As tiger caged. When I do set it free,
With angry fangs leaps on its prey. But see,
It now sleeps harmlessly, till Eblis calls
His faithful servant back. Lilith, when falls
The red fire at thy feet, dost fear?" "Nay, nay,"
She cried, and drew her white neck up. "A way
To tame it thou hast found. Believe me, since
It is thy slave I too will bind it, prince.
Should Lilith fear? Unfaltering, these eyes
Have watched when rushing storm-clouds heaped the skies,
And the black whirlwind, with loud, deafening roar,
Beat the torn waves; or whirled against the shore
The tumbling billows, with fierce lips that bit
The shrinking land. And the wreathed lightnings split
The cloud with thunder dread: or wildly burst
Upon the sea the water-spout. Shall first
She fear thy flame, who feared not these?" "Fit mate
Art thou for Eblis," answered he. "His fate
Share, great-souled one. Thou wouldst not meanly shrink,
Though his strong heart did fail. O Lilith, think!
The crown of clustered worlds thou mayest find,
If thou with him who loveth thee wilt bind
Thy life." "Nay, far happier seems to me
Than eagle caged, the wild lark soaring free,"
She said. And through her rose-pleached alleys strayed
They to the sea. And tender music made
That guileful voice; yet slow his wooing sped
Those summer days. But when were dead
And brown the crisping leaves, "Oh, love," he said,

"Of all the centuries, thou rarest bloom,
Thy shut heart open wide. Its sweet perfume,
Though I should die, fain would I parting drink.
Sleeps yet thy love? From me no longer shrink,
My Lilith. Oh, lift up thy tender eyes;
In their blue depths doth happy morning rise;
'Tis night if they be closed."
    She softly sighed;
And ancient strife recalling, thus replied:
"When dwelt a prince discrowned, well satisfied?
And fallen, loving, still art thou a prince,
And otherwhiles might sorrow bring me, since
It might hap thou wouldst much desire her realm,
Were Lilith thine; for princes seize the helm
When Love lies moored, and bid the shallop seek
Across the waves new lands. But Love is weak,
And so, alas, the craft upon the sands
Is dashed, while one, on-looking, wrings her hands.
Such days I have outlived. Like Adam, thou
Perchance will seek to bind the loosed. Then how
(If one hath drunken wine of liberty)
Shall she, athirst, rejoice; no longer free,
Be glad?"
    "My love," he said, "large-hearted lives,
Full dowers thee, and royal bounty gives,
Nor knoweth law, save Lilith's wish alone."
"Why, then," she answered, "on the polished stone
That fronts yon hill, write, Eblis, in full day,
That other time we read it clear, and say,
'Hereon are graven all those early vows
We whispered low aneath the summer boughs,'
Write every word. That so the stone shall be
Ever a witness mute twixt thee and me.
Then shall I know thou seekest in me no thrall
For after-days, if thou make compact. All
Thou hast said, write now."
    Then on the stone,
As she had said, graved Eblis, and thereon
Did set his seal. So wedded they: and hand

In hand the wide world roamed. Or in her land
Abode. And oft, of hours, ere yet on earth
He walked, she questioned. Or he loosed with mirth
Her yellow hair, down-streaming o'er his arm;
And 'gainst his cheek her breath came sweet and warm;
As through his dusky locks caressing played
Her fingers slim; and shadows, half afraid,
She saw in his wild eyes.
    Or paths remote
They trod, watching the white clouds rise and float
Athwart the sky. Or by the listless main,
Or 'neath the lotus bough, slow paced the twain.
Or dragon-trees spread their cool leafy screen.
And faint crept odors through the mangroves green,
Where paused the pair upon the sandy shore.
Love-tranced, unheeded, swiftly passed them o'er
Glad summer days: till one hour softly laid
At Lilith's feet a fair, lone babe, that strayed
From distant Dreamland far. So might one deem
That looked upon its face. Or, it might seem
From other climes, a rose-leaf blown apart,
Down-fluttered there, to gladden Lilith's heart.

Book IV

So that fair Elf-child other summers came;
But Lilith walked, heart-hungered, filled with shame,
Naught comforted. And in that shadow-land
She sorrowing bore, in after-time, a band
Of elfin babes, that waked dim echoes long
Forgotten there, and ghastly bursts of song.
Then Lilith saddened more, for that she knew
The curse was fallen now. And cried she through
Fast-falling tears, "Oh, me most desolate,
That shall not know in any time the fate
Of happier mothers! Nay, nor cool touch
Of baby hands. Oh, longed-for, loved so much!
Alas, my babes, ere yet hour-old ye fly,
Out-spreading shining wings with jeering cry,
Afar from me. Most hapless I, from whom
The crown of motherhood, yet white with bloom,
Falls blighted! Close in these empty arms fain
Would I clasp my babes! My tender pain
But once could ye not solace? Nay, 'tis vain;
I shall not kiss their lips, nor hear again,
As gladder mothers may, low-rippling, sweet,
The laughter children bring about their feet.
Oh, soulless ones, can ye not wait awhile,
'Till on your loveless lips I wake one smile?"
But merrily out-laughed the phantom crew;
On shining pinions white, swift seaward flew,
Or upward rose, slow-fading in the blue;
Or lured her trembling, green morasses through.
And 'mong the frothy waves they vanished fast;
Or shrieked with glee borne on the wintry blast,
And wilder raised their warlock song.

While fairer grew each day that elfin throng.

To pluck the mangoes brown, fair Lilith sped
One morn. Quick throbbed her heart. On mossy bed
Lay all her babes. With face like morning, shone
One there, and wide her yellow hair out-blown
As 'twere in play. Red-flushed her cheeks, and deep
About her lips the baby smiles. Asleep
Was one, white-gleaming, pure as pearl unseen
In sunless caves, close-shut. And one did lean
Against his fellow, lithe, sun-flushed and brown,
With rings of jetty hair that low adown
His bosom streamed. And one there was, whose dream
O'erflowed with laughter. And one did seem
Half-waking. One, with dimpled arms in sleep
Thrust elbow-deep in moss, that sure did weep
Ere yet he slept, and on his cheek scarce dried
The wilful tears.
    Then low, pale Lilith cried
As near she drew, down-bending tender eyes:
"And are ye here, my babes; and will ye rise
If I but break your sleep?" His naked feet
One faintly moved as low she leant; and warm
His slumbrous breath stirred 'gainst her circling arm,
And slow aneath his closed lids slipped a waft
Of wind, that loosed a trickling tear. Its craft
The mother-heart forgot thereat. "At last,
Close to my breast, my babes," she cried, and fast
Laughing, outstretched her eager hands and strong.
Then lay with empty arms.
    The elfin throng
Breasted the pulsing air with mocking song.
"Alas," she said, "could ye not give one kiss—
One tender clasp of hands! And must I miss
Your throbbing hearts from my cold, barren breast,
Ye soulless ones, that flout my lonely rest?"

There, prostrate, long lay Lilith, and there, late
'Mid dew-fall, Eblis found his stricken mate.
"O Eblis, say o'er me what curse hangs bare,

For now no more," she said, "this realm seems fair.
Its fruits grow bitter, all its light falls chill.
With thee, my prince, poor Lilith mates but ill—
Earth-born, with angel linked. Alas, is left
No joy to me, of my sweet ones bereft.
Methinks soft baby lips might erewhile drain
From Lilith's famished heart its wildest pain.
Wherefore, my Eblis, it were wise to seek
Surcease of grief. That Lilith, is so weak
Who wedded thee; and that she sinned, knew not.
Yet, if we part, mayhap may follow naught
Of other ills."

    "Sweet love," he laughed, "o'er-late
Thou art so timorous. At Eden's gate
Not so, what time the angel barred her way
My Lilith stood. Shelter within my arms. Oh, say,
Was not our young love sweet? Hath it grown cold?
With me thou sharest endless life; nor old,
Nor shrivelled, shalt thou be. And not one trace
Of earth's decay (sure doom of thy sad race)
Shall taint thy babes. For lo, I give
Thy soulless ones immortal youth. They live
Without a pang. And yet, methinks the cry
Of Earth adown the ages sounds, when die
Its babes; and mothers bend dumb lips above,
And fold still hands, that answer not their love.
Lilith, doth not indeed my love outweigh
Caresses missed from phantom babes? Astray
From Eden long, here in this fair domain
To bide; and through long cycles fearless reign
Methinks were joy. In summer sheen
Wide spreads thy land. The marge of islets green
The palm-trees skirt. Soft shine the dusk lagoons
And inland mountains. Mirk the jungle's glooms,
And fair thy fertile plains. Oh, sweet the glow
When we together watch the day, that low
Among the winds lies still. Shut lilies blow
While here we wait. Come, for they fain would show
Their golden hearts. Or, love, with me to float

Were it not sweet, through flowery bays remote,
Past coves and peaks? Or pierce yon ocean's verge,
And through wild tumbling waves our sails to urge?"
"Yea, sweet is love," she said, "and sweet to roam
By listless currents lulled; or 'mid the foam
Low dip our feathery oars," she sighed, "yet sore
Is still the mother-heart that hears no more
The lisping tongues. And sad, when baby smiles
Have left it desolate. And baby wiles
Shall cheer it never more."
    "Yet," Eblis said,
"Lilith, no longer mourn. For I have read
Upon a scroll as samite glistening white,
All coming fate, close hid from human sight,
Great peoples yet shall dwell in these dusk lands.
Then shall thy children, shadowy bands
That fly thy fond caress, with them abide
In closest fellowship. And though they hide
Sometimes from human ken their better selves,
Still loved, remain these tricksy elves.
Though yet indeed some quips and pranks they play,
'Tis but a jest, men know, when far away
The flickering marsh-fires swift they light
And children follow their false tapers bright
Among the spongy bogs. The ship-lad smiles,
When distant 'mid the waves the phantom isles
Rise green. 'Tis but a harmless jest that sets
On lonely plains, domes, mosques, and minarets,
And o'er the desert sands, mirage uplifts
When glimmering waves shine through deep rifts
Of crested palms.
    "Still dearer they when wide
To undiscovered lands men boldly ride
Across new seas, and turn their venturous prows.
When tempests shriek, and wet about their brows
The salt spray dashes fierce, one, watching, cries,
'Good mates, no storm I fear, for yonder rise
The Elf-babes 'mid the foam. Ye goblin crew,
That sail these unknown seas, we follow you

To harbor safe. Ho, ho! With beckoning hands,
Wind-driven, loud they cry—My mates! the lands,
The golden lands we seek, are ours!'
     "In Earth's brown bosom pent, the hardy wight
Long in deep caverns dwells; and hard doth smite
The rocky caves. Nor sees the golden spoil
Through weary days of wasted, lonely toil.
From his wild eyes, far-flying hides the prize,
Till desperate, angered, worn, aloud he cries:
'Vain, vain! The caves my labor answer not,
Nor yellow threads, that gleam in any grot.
Hard, cruel, silent hills, my strength ye mock,
And seal your treasures close in flinty rock;
So, after toilsome years, sweet wife, I bring
To thee no sparkling love-gift. Nay, nor anything
To cheer our failing time.'
     "Then round him hears
He sturdy blows, and listening, almost fears
He dreams. But swift the echoes rise, and still
More loudly roll, and quick replies the hill.
Reverberant, through all the caverns round,
The uproar swells, and fills the world with sound.
Then lists he once again. 'With lusty shocks
Your hammers ring against the hard-ribbed rocks—
Goblins!' he boldly shouts, 'smite! smite! ye bring
My treasure forth, dark-beating goblin wing
Among the gleaming caves, whose dusk veins hold
The gold. At last! At last, the ruddy gold!'

"And lone, in stricken fields, the husbandman
Sits pale, with anxious eyes that hopeless scan
The burning sky. Hot lie the glimmering plain
And uplands parched. 'Behold, the bending grain,
Fair in the springtide, now is dead; and dry
The brooks. If yet the rainfall fail, we die
Of famine sore. No bleating lambs I hear in fold
Safe shut, nor lowing kine; nor on the wold
The whir of mounting bird: Nor thrives about me
Any living thing. So seemeth, end must be
Of striving. Since all the land is cursed,

What matter if by famine scorched, or thirst,
We die?' he saith.
    "And thick the warlock swarm
Above his head, wide-spreading dark wings warm,
Fast flitted by. The waiting fields he stands
Among. And laughing, claps exultant hands.
'Good speed ye, Sprites! that bring the welcome cloud
And pile the vapors thick,' he shouts aloud.
Oh! sweet shall bloom again the bending grain,
And clothe afresh the wide, the wasted plain.
The clouds sweep black. Ha, ha! Against my cheek
The big drops fall. Merry the goblins shriek.
Behold, they mount, they sink, they rise again.
Ho, friendly elves, that bring the longed-for rain!'"

Thereat, he, smiling, ceased. And when soft crept
The listening stars across the sky, they slept
Untroubled, 'neath the mango-trees.
    But when midway
The night was spent, Prince Eblis waking lay.
Soft Lilith's breathing 'mong the droopt leaves stirred.
And he, sore troubled, mused on every word
That Lilith spake ere yet they slept. In all
Foreseeing much of ill that might befall
Their love. "O, queenly soul! Of finer grain
Thou art than angels are. And more in brain
Than man, I hold thee. Sooth, yet taints thee still
One touch of womankind. And since so chill
She finds her babes, must I forego my vow?
For one flaw, Hope's clear crystal break? Oh, how
Ally her cause with mine! So doth she long
For human love—a baby hand is strong
To hurl my empire down. From her soft heart
Red, baby lips can drain revenge, and start
Unbidden tears. And pity wakes to life
When 'mong dead embers she sits lone, and strife
Is done.
    "Then, at Regret's dull heels, lo, fast,
Retrieving follows. Happy days long past
She will recall. If so for love she yearn,

Back to her early home once more will turn,
Pardoning her wilful lord. And he again
Shall win the woman I so love, and fain
Would hold forever. Lilith, thou one balm
Of my lost soul in all this world! Shall calm
My sufferings, or love me, any one, save thee,
When thou in Adam's arms forgettest me?
My only love! Nay, then, 'twere surely wise
To shut these baby faces from her eyes,
New seeds of wrath to sow, her hate so feed
That all her rankling wounds afresh shall bleed.
And in her ears 'Good Adam!' will I cry,
Lest she forget Eden she lost thereby.
Yea, 'Adam!' I will laugh. Till her red lips with guile
O'erflow. And she shall curse him loud. With subtlest wile
Safe won, then shall she ever be mine own.
Soul-bound to me in hate, more terrible than death
In hate, that long outlasts Love's puny breath—
O cunning craft, that with the self-same blow
Forever wins my love, and smites my foe!

"Last night, when Lilith slept, lest I might mar
Her dreams, from our green couch I rose, and far
Passed silent. Know I not the spell that draws
My feet unwilling, Edenward. Its laws
I may not brave to rend my foe. Nor there
The Angel pass, unseen. The night so fair,
As prone among the glistening leaves I lay,
On Adam shone. Not sad, as on a day
Erstwhile he seemed. And I could almost swear
The sound of silvery laughter on the air
Fell soft. And a fleet footfall 'mong the flowers
Scattered the dew. Yet 'mid those silent bowers
Naught else I saw or heard save rippling flow
Of waters, and the moonshine white. Oh, low
Speak, Eblis, lest aloud the night may tell
Thy secret to the stars. Yet it were well
If lies the hidden cure for Lilith's woe
Close shut in Paradise.
        "All would we know,

If we, close hid without those verdant walls,
Together watched. What fate soe'er befalls
I care not, if with me she bide."
    Down bent
He o'er her hair, thick with the night-dew sprent.
Soft kissed it, crying, "Love, the morn shines bright.
Waken, my Lilith, now. Through lands of night
Our happy course afar doth ever wend;
Past smiling shores where mighty rivers bend,
Past cove and cape and isle, and winding bay
And still blue mists, that hang athwart the day."
Thereat she rose, and joyously they sped
By broad lagoons where musky odors shed
New blooms. About them coiled long wreaths of vine,
And slim lianas drooped, and marish lichens fine.
And fared they on o'er many a slanting beach
And mountain crest; past many an open reach
And forest wild—till over Paradise
They saw the stars, clear, tender, loving, rise.
Then 'neath the screen of those rose-girdled walls
They hid without, listing the waterfalls,
Or bird belated, twittering to its nest.
So still the spot, the very grass to rest
Seemed hushed.
    The garden-close, a clinging rose o'ercrept.
Its lustrous stem without that drooping swept
Thick set with buds as tintless as the snows
On sunless hills, when wild the north wind blows.

Lilith a-tiptoe stood; upreaching, caught
The swaying boughs. Her eyes with longing fraught
Close scanned her old deserted home. Then came
Upon her spirit sadness, as if blame
Unuttered breathed through those remembered glades
And touched the odors moist 'mong mirky shades.
With wistful gaze, she traced each bosky dell,
Each winding path. And sweet youth's memories fell
About her.
    Then was she ware of Adam, slow
Pacing the pleasance-ways. With ruddy glow

Fresh shone his cheeks, and crisp his hair out-blown
By wanton winds. His lips were mirthful grown.
Once he made pause hard by the coppice green
That hid the watcher. Once the leafy screen
So near he passed, from the overhanging edge
He brushed a rose. The hindering hedge
Quick through, in sudden blessing slim white hand
Fain had she reached. "O Eden mine! Dear land,"
She sighed. And springing warm the tender tide
Of teardrops gemmed the roses at her side.

So greets the weary wanderer once more
His early home. The lintels worn, the door
Age-stained; the iris clumps, in sheltered nook;
The mill-wheel rotting o'er the shrunken brook;
The sunny orchard, sloping west; and far
And cold, above his mother's grave, a star—
Then quick unbidden tears, the heart's warm rain,
O'erflow his soul, and leave it pure again.
So Lilith backward turned to holier days,
Watching through misty tears where trod those ways
Her feet in other times.
    Sudden and sweet
Came down those paths a glimpse of flying feet;
A sound of girlish laughter smote the air.
In jealous rage, Lilith uprose to dare
The guarding Angel's wrath. But, silver clear,
The mocking laugh of Eblis caught her ear.
"Thou hast forgot," he said, "this peaceful land,
Living, thou canst not enter."
    But her hand
Grasped once again the roses' shining strand,
And 'neath her guileful touch, like scarlet flame
The snowy flowers burned. So, first Earth's shame
Around them set the spikèd thorns.
    Long there
Pale Lilith looked, as coldly still and fair
As carven stone. Then, with a fierce despair,
A sense of utter loss, downbending there,
With fingers hot she tore the hedge apart

And laid thereto her face. With sorer smart
She gazed again. For now, the twain at rest
Were laid. Pure as a dream, Eve's sinless breast
A babe close pressed. One pink foot, small and warm,
Among the leaves was hid. One dimpled arm
Aneath her head.
    Low Eblis sneered. "I wot
In young Eve's arms my Lilith is forgot.
Oh, soon," he said, "these earth-worms changeful turn—
From the oped rose when red the shut buds burn."
But wild eyes on the babe she fixed. "Oh, blind,"
She cried, "was I. Yea, if the wanton wind
Doth mock, I will not chide. Was it for this
I wandered far, and bartered Eden's bliss?
For this have lost the very bloom of life?
So Adam comfort finds, not knowing strife!
Look you, that fragile thing at Adam's side—
I heed her not. But Lilith is denied
The treasure she so careless doth possess.
See how the babe, scarce waking, doth caress
The mother! Look! Oh, hear the mother croon
Above her child! Ah, Eblis, love, I swoon—
I shall not know such joy. Alas, to me
No babe shall come! Accurséd may she be,
Cursed Adam too. Thrice heavy on the head
Of this poor babe my wrong be visited."
So, trembling, she brake off.
    "Fast fades the light,
Sweet love. Once more to our dark realm of night
Let us return," he said.
    As on fared they
With merry jest, Eblis gan cheer the way.
"Nay, otherwhiles mirth pleased," she said. "Knowest thou
What name she bears, who dwells in Eden now?
When Lilith went, long tarried Adam lone?"
She said. Replied he, "All to me is known
Since that same hour you parted. What befell,
To thee as we wend onward I will tell.

"Calm morn in Eden streaked the skies with red,

And flushed the waiting hills above the grassy bed
Where Adam, joyless, saw new rise the sun,
Unwinding golden webs night-vapors spun
Athwart low meads. Slow, droning murmurs sent
The waking bees, with bloom and fragrance blent.
Unheeded poured her music blithesome Day
The reedy brooks beside and shallows gray.
For lone to Adam seemed the place, and cold;
The landscape dumb, as one aneath the mould.
For Lilith's sake, no more was Eden fair.
Bloomless the days, the nights bowed down with care.
Oft pacing pathways dim, he saw the gleam
Of strange-faced flowers beside the purling stream,
Or toyed with circling leaves; or plucked the grass,
And watched through rifted trees the clouds o'erpass;
Wide roaming, heard the waters idly break
Far 'gainst the curving beach.

    "And grieving, spake,
'Oh, sweet with thee each hour—each wilding way,
And sweet the memory of each gathered spray.
Could you not wait, dear love? Or come once more?
Yea, 'till you come, vain doth great Nature pour
Her richest gifts.' He paused, and heard alone
Respondent fall, the wood-dove's plaintive moan,
And the spent winds among the scented glades.
Moss-couched beneath the glinting forest shades,
He gazed, when shadows o'er the hills crept light,
Quick vanishing, like phantom fingers white,
Until on mead, and mere, and sounding shore
Eden found voice, sad plaining, 'Never-more!'
Long time he pondered on blue peaks remote
When slow, as stranded ships that listless float,
Moved by the sunset clouds. Or the white rack
Swept o'er the garden walls.

    "'Would I their track
Might take,' he said, 'Lilith, so long you stay.
Whom my soul follows sorrowing—alway.'
Thus ever mourned he, comfortless; that so
In after days the Master, in the glow

Of morning-tide, the mother of the race
Gave for his solacement.
    "Oh, fair the face
Young Eve bent o'er his sleep. Ere down the glade
The startled fawn leaps swift, her glance dismayed
Questions the hunter, mute. Such eyes—so brown,
So soft, so winning, shy—that looked adown
When Adam waked. Like vagrant tendrils, tossed
Dark hair about her brows. And quaintly crossed
Her hands upon her breast. Less red the dart
That deepest cleaves the folded rose's heart,
Than her round cheeks. Not hers the regal air
Of Lilith lost, the white arms, lissom, bare,
The slender throat; the elbows dimpled deep, whereto
Might scarcely reach Eve's head.
    "Yet soft, as through
Some pleasant dream, the summer's spicy air
Stirs odorous 'mong seaward gardens fair,
In southland hid; so, gently, Eve straightway
To Adam's life unbidden came, to stay
Forever there. Sure entrance then made she
Into that heart untenanted by thee.
"So, to some olden house, from whose shut doors
One went erewhile, another comes. Its floors
All empty sees. The lowly threshold worn,
The moss-grown roof, the casements left forlorn.
Amid the shadows round about him stands,
Missing the footsteps passed to other lands,
And whispers tenderly, 'Since here no more
The owner bides, what harm if on the floor
I pass? Good chance it were the clambering vine
About the porch with fingers deft to twine—
To draw the curtains, ope the door. For who
May know how soon these paths untended, through,
He comes again, with weary, way-worn feet,
Who made aforetime, other days so sweet.
Wherefore, I enter now. For whose dear sake
These vacant rooms, white, fragrant, clean, I make.
And when, world-wearied, he returns, we twain

Perchance together bide. Nor part again.'
So Eve found refuge. Tender love, the spell
Whereby she ruled. Peaceful the pair did dwell.
Fast fled the happy years, till softly laid
In her glad arms the babe—a winsome maid."
He ended there. Between them silence deep
Fell, as they journeyed. And the furthest steep
They crossed, that o'er their shadow-world rose high.
Then saw they level plains, their home, anigh.
And now, seeking her pleasance once again,
They came to their own land. But all in vain
His care. Silent she was, and oft did grieve,
Till Eblis wrathful cried: "Because this Eve
Adam holds dear, art mourning? Still dost yearn
To mate his sordid soul? Or wouldst thou turn
From summer land to Eden walls?

"The man
Belike, ne'er loved thee. So is it young Eve can
His pulses sway. Is she not passing fair?
Her fancies wild, it is her daily care
To bend beneath his ever fickle will.
Red-lipped and soft, she deftly rules him still,
Though he wist not. Yet sweeter Lilith's frown
Than archest smile she wears. Great Soul! The crown
Thou bearest of fadeless life. For fleeting dreams
In Paradise, beside the winding streams,
Wilt thou resign such boon? Thou art, in sooth,
Of mold too firm for Adam's love. In truth
A prince—though fallen—consorts best with thee
Say which were wise, with Eden's lord to be,
Or, shining high, the purer soul, the star
That fadeless burns, and Eblis lights afar?
Were it not grand through endless spaces hurled
With me to drive, above a shrinking world
Our chariot, wide?

"For I foresee when dawn
Dark days upon our foes, and hope is gone.
Wherefore, my Lilith, now, as seems thee good,
Make choice." Thereat she, turning where she stood,

With kisses hung about his neck, and smiled,
Crying, "Thine, Eblis, thine!" So were they reconciled.

Book V

And Lilith oft to Paradise returned,
For fierce within her, bitter hatred burned,
And better, dearer, seemed revenge than aught
She else desired. The coppice oft she sought,
Much hoping direful evil might be wrought
Upon the love that bloomed in Eden.
    Wide
Oft strayed fair Eve; the little maid, beside,
Plucking the lotus; or by sedgy moats,
From ribbed papyrus broad, frail fairy boats
Deft fashioning. Or Adam, watching, smiled,
With flowery wreaths engarlanding the child.
And laughed the pair, intent on pleasant toil,
When blithe the child upheaped her fruity spoil—
Great globes of red and gold. Or roguish face
O'er feathery broods, or in the further space
To count the small blue eggs, she sportive bent;
And far her restless feet swift glancing went.
It chanced one day she watched the careless flight
Of vagrant butterflies, that circled light
Uncertain, high, above a copse rose-wreathed;
Then soft down-dropping, gaudy wings they sheathed
Beside a darkling pool. The copse anear
With yellow buds was strewn. And softly here
She crept, deeming her little half-shut hand
Might snare the fairest of that gleaming band.
Yet ere she touched it, wide its wings outspread
In flight.
    And still she, swift pursuing, sped
Among the groves, till wearied, slept the maid
Deep in the mid-day shadows, lowly laid.

Without, stooped Lilith. And with fingers swift,
Among the leaves she oped a small green rift,
That she might see the child. The hedge was wet
With starry blooms. Whereto her hand she set
When she awaked, seeing each dainty frond
Of fragrant ferns, dusk mirrored in the pond.
The child came near the copse, much wondering:
From glossy stems the smooth leaves sundering.
And stooping o'er the rift, she saw there, low
Against the hedge, a face like drifted snow,
And soft eyes, blue as violets show
Above the brooks; and hair that downward rolled
Upon the ground in glittering strands of gold.
Mute stood the maid, naught fearing, but amazed.
Then nearer drew, and lingering, she gazed
In those blue orbs. And smiling as she knelt,
The stranger quickly loosed her shining belt
Of gems. Flawless each stone whose pallid gleam
Lit silent nooks, or slept by far-off stream
Unheeded—pale pearls with shimmering light,
From distant oceans plucked, blue sapphires bright,
And diamonds rosy-cold, and burning red
The rubies fine, and yellow topaz shed
Its sultry glow, jasper, dull onyx white,
Sardonyx, rare chalcèdon, streaked with light.
Against her white breast that bright zone she laid,
Then stretched it, flashing forth, toward the maid,
And clasped it round her throat.
     A luring strain
She sung, sweet as the pause of summer rain.
So soft, so pure her voice, the child it drew
Still nearer that green rift; and low there-through
She laughing stroked the down-bent golden head
With her soft baby hands. And parting, spread
The silken hair about her little face,
And kissed the temptress through the green-leaved space.
Whereat fell Lilith snatched the babe and fled,
Crying, as swift from Eden's bounds she sped,
And like a fallen star shone on her breast

The child, "At last! at last! thy peaceful rest
Ere long will cease. O helpless mourn, frail Eve,
Uncomforted. O hapless mother, grieve,
Since Lilith far from thee thy babe doth bear!
She leaves thy loving arms, thy tender care.
Nor canst thou follow anywhere my flight,
When far we go athwart the falling night.
Ah, little babe, close-meshed in yellow hair
Thou liest pale! Fear not, thou art so fair,
Much comfort lives in thee."
    So ended she,
And onward, hostile lands among, passed fleet
Blue solitudes afar, till paused her feet,
Where highest 'mong hoar climbing peaks, uprose
A mountain crest.
    It was the third day's close.
In those untrodden ways there was no sound,
No sight of living thing, the barren heights around.
No hum of insect life, no whirring wing of bird.
Bare rocks alone, all fissured, blotched and blurred
As with red stain of battle-fields unseen.
Far, far below, still vales were shining green.
And leaping downward swift, a mountain stream
Crept soft to sleep, where meadow grasses dream.
Wan, wayworn, there, the babe upon her knee,
Lilith sat down. "O Eve," she said, "on me
The child smiles sweet! Fondle her silken hair
If now thou canst, or clasp her small hands fair.
Thou hast my Paradise. Lo, thine I bear
Afar from thee. See, then! Its transient woe
Thy babe e'en now forgets; and sweet and low
It babbles on my knee. In sooth, not long
Endure her griefs, and through my crooning song
She kisses me, recalling not the place
Whence she has come. Nay, nor her mother's face."
Long time stayed Lilith in that land. More calm
Each day she grew, for soft, like healing balm,
The child's pure love fell on her sin-sick soul.
Now oft among the crags, fleet-footed, stole

The maid, or lightly crossed the fertile plain.
And blithesome sang among the growing grain
That brake in billowy waves about her feet.
But when the wheat full ripened was, and sweet,
She plucked and ate. Thereat a shadowy pain,
A sense of sorrow, stirred that childish brain,
She wist not why. For it did surely seem
Before her waking thought, with pallid gleam
Of other days, dim pictures passed; of wood
And stream, beyond these mountain rims. And stood,
It seemed, midway a garden wide, a tree that bright
Like silver gleamed, and broad boughs light
Uplifted. Like ripened wheat the fruit thereon,
When low the westering sun upon it shone.
Then slow the maid did turn, and silent stand
At Lilith's side. And o'er that mountain land,
Down-looking, mused. Or lifted pensive eyes,
And gaze that questioned if in any wise
She might perceive the land she longing sought;
But of its stream, or garden, saw she naught.
Thereat Lilith with white lips drew more near,
And clasped in her lithe arms the child so dear.
And once again fled swift, a shadowy shape,
Across green fields. And heard, through silence, break
A voice she could not hush, that loudly wailed,
"My babe! Give me my babe!"
    And Lilith paled,
And listening, heard, borne ever on the wind,
The tread of feet fast following behind.
Then westward turned, where once among new ways
With Eblis she had trod in other days,
When far they wandered. Thitherward she bent
Her timid steps, the babe upon her breast,
Until with travel worn her noontide rest
She took. And now a land of alien blooms
About them lay, outwafting strange perfumes.
And quaint defiles, that sloped behind a bay;
And level fields; and curly vines that lay
Thick clustered o'er with unripe fruit; and bent

Above them fragrant limes and spicy scent
Of citron and of myrtle all the place
Made sweet, and 'mid the trees, an open space
    They saw.
Not far away a broad lagoon
Burned like a topaz 'neath a crescent moon,
For day was parting. Even-tide apace
Drew on, and chill the night dews filled the place.
Upon the waters dusky shadows clung,
And ashen-gray the broad leaves drooping hung;
Low 'mong the marish buds lay one that made
Against the sudden dusk a duskier shade—
Despairing arms upflinging to the sky,
Smiting the silence with unheeded cry—
"O mother, childless! Wife—of all bereft!
Alas, my babe, not even thou art left
To comfort me, in these last hopeless days,
Shut out from Paradise. Through unknown ways
I sought thee sorrowing. Oh, once again,
My Adam, come! Is not this gnawing pain
Of punishment enow, that thou unkind
Art grown? Ah, never more shall I thee find?
Alas, I ever was but weak. Alone
I cannot live. Come but again, mine own.
No longer leave me mourning, desolate.
In tears I call thee. Oh, in tears I wait
Thy sweet, forgiving kiss!"
    Ended she so
Her plaint. And 'mong the glistening leaves hid low,
Lilith yet fiercer clasped the child
When that lorn mother, tear-stained, weeping, wild,
Poured forth her woe.
As one that wakes to life
From peaceful dreams, leaps quick amid the strife
Of morning hours, so now the maid to pass
From Lilith's arms strove hard. And loosed her clasp,
And turned her shadowed face with plaintive moan
And fond beseeching eyes, where lay her mother lone.
But Lilith hardening, seized the child again,

And from her ears shut out the mother's pain
With wilful hands.
    So passed she quick away.
Across the dusky path, low fallen, lay
Pale Eve, till clear she saw the dawn's pure ray,
And as she looked, the voice of one she heard
Anigh. Her heart to sudden joy was stirred.
"Rise up, mine own," he said, "no more apart
We walk." Then she arose, and cried, "Dear heart,
Close hold me. So! Methinks I dreamed we were
Parted long time."
    So went, the exiled pair
From home thrust out, together—everywhere.
And oft they journeyed on with sufferings spent
To distant lands. And oft with labor bent
Recalled the olden home, with brimming eyes,
Hemmed in by mountains blue—lost Paradise.

Meanwhile, to her own realm Lilith long since
Was come, glad greeting Eblis. "O my prince,
I have most bravely done. Our foes full sore
Are smitten now. My guerdon o'er and o'er
Thou wilt bestow, I ween, in kisses warm
As my own southland's breath. For I great harm
Have wrought that hated pair. With feeble moan
Lies Eve in a far land, thrust out. Alone,
Deserted. And whence angered Adam flies
I know not. Nay, nor what new world his eyes
Behold. Nor even if he live.
    "But see!
Sleeps on my breast the babe—Eve's babe. And she
Shall know no more its tender, sweet caress,
Soft medicining woe. The wilderness
Uncheered by love, is hers."
    And by the sea,
Peaceful abode, long time content, the three,
Save that the child unmurmuring drooped.
Then oft above her Lilith, singing, stooped,
Striving to wake the baby smiles again
About her wee, warm mouth. Vain wiles! And vain

Her loving skill. All still she lay, and pale.
As one at sea pines for a lonely vale
Besprent with cuckoo flowers; the faint wild breath
Of cradled buds, among the cloven elms, and saith,
'I shall not see that place beyond the seas,
Nor any more pluck red anemones
In windless nooks.'
    So seemed the child, and frail
As one that weeps above dead joys. Then pale
Grew Lilith as those wasting lips she pressed
And kissed the filmy eyes, and kissing, blessed
The child.
    But Eblis touched the hand so worn,
The faded, wasted face. "Happy, thou mother lorn,
Unseeing her," he said. "This fragile thing
To-day lies on thy breast. To-morrow's wing
Hath brushed it from thy sight." Low Lilith sighed:
"My Eblis, is this death?" And louder cried,
"But thou art wise, and sure some hidden way
From this sore hap canst find. O Eblis, say,
Hast thou no spell whereby the child may live?
O love, my realm thy recompense I give,
If she be healed."
    "Nay; not Archangel's craft
Stays fleeting life, or turns Death's nimble shaft,"
He said. "Yet if," she mused, "I laid again
The child in young Eve's arms, like summer rain,
The mother's love may yet restore again
This shriveled life. And yet, must I resign
The babe? Alas, my little one! Nay, mine
No more!" Weeping she ceased.
    But after, bore
The child far northward; the exiled pair o'er
Many lands long seeking. Till from a crest
Of barren hills Lilith looked down. At rest,
The twain she saw, for it was eventide.
And low they spoke of hidden snares beside
Their unknown path, since unaware fared they
Into this hostile spot. The dim wolds lay

All bare beneath chill stars. And far away
Were belts of pine, and dingy ocean shore,
Like wrinkled lip. Cold was the land, and hoar
With wintry rime. Near by, its leafless boughs
A thorn bush bent, with withered berries red.
At sight thereof Adam, rejoicing, said,
"My Eve, bide here. From yonder friendly tree
The ripe fruit I will pluck and bring to thee."
"Oh, leave me not! This solitude I fear;
The land about is chill," she said, "and drear
It seems to me." But Adam answered, "Nay,
Sore famished art thou, and not far away
It is—nor long I stay."
    So parted he.
Not long alone was Eve. Upstarted she
Dismayed. A woman, most exceeding fair,
Beside her stood, with coils of yellow hair,
And blue eyes, calm as sleep among the hills'
Dim lakes. Eve, frighted, shrank. As mountain rills,
Sweet fell the stranger's words. "My sister, one
Is here that glad salutes thee. And since done
Is now my quest, and here my journey ends,
I bring a goodly gift. For elsewhere wends
My pathway, Eve.
    "Beside a coppice green,
Brighter than gold, purer than silver sheen,
In a fair garden, once a jewel shone.
With it, compared in all the world, no stone.
And low the Master set it shining clear
Against the hedge, saying, 'When she draws near
She will perceive on whom I do bestow
This moteless gem, that fellow doth not know.'
    "Now I without the copse that day was hid.
Soft shone the jewel, as the moon amid
The blue. And in the garden I saw thee,
Where in the midst stood a fair wheaten tree
As emerald green. Its ears, as rubies red,
Fragrant as breath of musk, its odors spread.
And white its shining grains as rifted snow.

I looked again. And in thy fair hand, lo,
Full ripe bright gleamed the yellow wheaten grain.
Thou saidst, 'Though I did eat, I live. No pain
Hath marred this pleasant feast.'
    "Then I the more
Desired thy gem. 'All things most goodly pour
On Eve their gifts. But I am famished lone,'
I said. And still against the hedge the stone
Rayed like a frozen tear the pure Night shed—
The which with trembling hand I seized, and fled
Afar.
    "But now upon my soul weighs sore
A dream. A voice called loud, 'Straightway restore
To Eve that which is hers; lest I, that bright
Set it against the hedge, will quench its light.
Yea, I will crumble it and quickly smite
It into dust e'en from thy hand.' Mine eyes
I careless closed. But yesternight 'Arise!'
The stern voice cried. 'Stay not at all. For lo,
I wait not. Lest I scourge thee sorely, go!'
Ah, Eve, though long upon my heart I wore
This jewel rare, behold, I now restore
Thine own!"
    Then Eve cried loud, "Ere my heart break,
Give me my babe! Where is she, for whose sake
I sorrowed all these years—the little maid?"
She said, through tender sobs.
    And Lilith laid
Apart upon her breast her garment, dyed
In blended hues. And stooping at Eve's side,
Gave back the child.
    As one that ending quest
Most perilous, safe harbor sees—at rest
Among green hills—and enters glad therein,
So Lilith was.
    So passed she once again
Into her land.
    But Eve, like rain
Long pent, upon the child poured swiftly down

Sweet kisses. And again, twixt laugh and frown
Divided, smoothed the baby face, and through
Her fingers soft the silken hair she drew,
And kissed again.

    And with a vague surprise
Recalled the stranger's smile, the mournful eyes,
Much marveling whence she fared. And said, "As pale
She seemed as bramble-blooms in Eden's vale."

When homeward Adam came, the child she set
Upon his knee, saying, "Erewhile I met
An angel. So to me she seemed, as there
She stood. So tall, so yellow-haired, so fair;
And lo, she brought again the babe."

    Therewith
She ended low. "Doubtless an angel, love, sith
So you deem her," he replied. And mused on all
Eve told.

    And watching, saw a shadow fall
Upon the child. And later, did recall
Those words, sad pondering "so fair, so tall."
But nothing uttered.

    In that land long time
They lingered. And the child slow faded, till
One day Eve frighted cried, "See, Adam, still
She lies! Ah, little one, unseal those eyes!
Rouse but awhile, ere waning daylight flies!"
For she discerned not yet its doom, nor knew
The hour was near.

    But Adam, parting, drew
Beneath the thorn, lest he might see the child.
And all the lone hours through Eve, babbling, smiled
Adown. And blew her warm breath o'er the cheeks
So wan. "The night grows cold," she said. "Sleep creeps
Dull on my babe. The night grows cold and chill,"
She said.

    Nor dreamed aneath those lids closed still,
The death film hung.

    A wind uprose, and swept
Among the dry leaves heaped, where lowly slept

The child. Cold grew the night and colder, till
Against the east the dawn glowed daffodil,
Above dun wolds white with new-fallen snow.
So rose the day and widened into morning glow
With rosy tints o'erstreaked, and faintly blurred
With flecks of cloud.
    Still lay the child, nor stirred.
Dumb Eve looked down, nor knew Death's pallid masque,
And strove to wake the maid. In vain. Her task
Was done. And as she gazed, a gentle grasp
Soft loosed the dead from that cold mother's clasp,
And Lilith laid the babe in its chill bed—
Straightened the limbs, and kissed the little head.
And o'er the sleeper, kneeling, she did lean.
Forth from her breast she drew, close folded, green,
A sheath of leaves, bright shining, lustrous—wet
With tears—that in those waxen hands she set.
Then those shut leaves oped slow. And low and frail
Bloomed 'mid the tintless snows a snow-drop pale.
Soft Lilith said, "For this pale sleeper's sake,
O Eve, one kiss bestow. E'en thou canst take
Pity on me. For thee new, happy days await,
But I—I am forever desolate.
For thee fresh love will bloom above this mould;
For thee, in coming years, pure lips unfold;
But I—no more, no more, shall feel the warm
Breath 'gainst my breast. Nay, nor the baby arm
Soft clasping me. Nor see the feet that pass
Like falling music, through the waving grass.
Therefore, one pardoning kiss give e'er I go
To my own land, beyond this realm of snow."
And Eve, uprising, took the hand she gave,
And weeping, kissed; and parted by that grave.

Stood Adam, after-time, by that small mound.
Low at their feet a sheaf of leaves Eve found,
Wherein white flowers shone. "Oh, like," she said,
"To this was one abloom within the bed
Where lies the child. And fair, O, passing fair,
She was, and tall, with yellow gleaming hair,

And cheeks soft flushed as fresh pomegranate bells;
And dewy eyes, like violets in the dells,
Who came. So, silent passed that stranger fair
Who loved our babe. And e'er I well was ware,
She vanished."
     Otherwhiles, "Of alien race
She was," Eve said. "A princess, with a face
Surpassing fair, who trod the pathway bright
Among the mists, beyond the rim of night
To her own land."
     And oft in after-time,
When Cain had lain in her young arms, and chime
Of voices round her came, and clasp of hands,
And thick with baby faces bloomed the lands,
Eve silent sat, remembering that one child
Among the snowdrops, in a Northern wild.
And Lilith dwelt again in her own land;
With Eblis still strayed far. And hand in hand
They talked; the while her phantom brood in glee
Laughed overhead. Then looking on the sea,
Low voiced, she sang. So sweet the idle song,
She said, "From Paradise, forgotten long,
It comes. An elfin echo that doth rise
Upward from summer seas to bending skies.
In coming days, from any earthly shore
It shall not fail. And sweet forever more
Shall make my memory. That witching strain
Pale Lilith's love shall lightly breathe again.
And Lilith's bitter loss and olden pain
O'er every cradle wake that sweet refrain.
My memory still shall bloom. It cannot die
While rings Earth's cradle-song—sweet lullaby."

Slow passed dim cycles by, and in the earth
Strange peoples swarmed; new nations sprang to birth.
Then first 'mong tented tribes men shuddering spake
Dread tales of one that moved, an unseen shape,
'Mong chilling mists and snow. A spirit swift,
That dwelt in lands beyond day's purple rift.
Phantom of presage ill to babes unborn,

Whose fast-sealed eyes ope not to earthly morn.
"We heard," they cried, "the Elf-babes shrilly scream,
And loud the Siren's song, when lightnings gleam."
Then they that by low beds all night did wake,
Prayed for the day, and feared to see it break.

When o'er the icy fjords cold rise white peaks,
And fierce wild storms blot out the frozen creeks,
The Finnish mother to her breast more near
Draws her dear babe—clasps it in her wild fear
Still closer to her heart. And o'er and o'er
Through her weird song fall echoes from that lore
That lived when Time was young, e'er yet the rime
Of years lay on his brow. In that far prime
Nature and man, couched 'neath God's earliest sky,
Heard clear-voiced spheres chant Earth's first lullaby.
Now, in the blast loud sings the Finn, and long,
Nor knows that faint through her wild cradle-song
Yet sweetly thrills the vanished Elf-babes' cry,
Nor dreams, as low she croons her lullaby,
Still breathes through that sweet, lingering refrain
Lilith the childless—and to life again,
To love, she wakes.
    The soft strain clearer rings
As through the gathering storm that mother sings:

    Pile the strong fagot,
    Pale Lilith comes!
Wild through the murky air goblin voices shout.
Hark! Hearest thou not their lusty rout?
    Lilith comes!
    Listen, my babe!

    See how the dusk pines
    Tremble and crouch;
Over wide wastes borne, white are the snow-wreaths blown,
And loud the drear icy fjords shudder and moan;
    Lilith comes!
    Listen, my babe!

    Ah! Hear the wild din,

>   Fierce o'er the linn,
> The sea-gull, affrighted, soars seaward away,
> And dark on the shores falls the wind-driven spray;
>   Lilith comes!
>   Listen, my babe!
>
>   The shuddering ice
>   Shivers. It cracks!
> Like a wild beast in pain, it cries to the wrack
> Of the storm-cloud overhead. The sea answers back—
>   Dread Lilith comes!
>   Listen, my babe!
>
>   Near draws the wraith fair,
>   Dull gleams her hair.
> Ah, strong one, so cruel—fierce breath of the North—
> The torches of heaven are lighting thee forth!
>   Fell Lilith comes!
>   Listen, my babe!
>
>   Cold spirit of Snow,
>   Ah, I fear thee!
> The sports of my hunter, the white fox, the bear,
> The spoils of our rivers are thine. Ah, then spare,
>   Dread Lilith, spare
>   The babe at my breast!
>
>   Mercy, weird Lilith!
>   Even sleeping,
> My babe lies so chill. See, the reindeer I give!
> Ah, lift thy dark wings, that my darling may live!
>   Pale Lilith comes!
>   Listen, my babe!
>
>   Once, in the Northland,
>   Pale crocus grew
> By half-wakened stream. It lay shriveled and low
> Ere the spring-time had come, in soft shroud of snow.
>   Sad Lilith comes!
>   Listen, my babe!

      Foul Vampire, drain not
      From my loved one
The life-current red. O Demon, art breaking
My heart while I plead? Ah, babe! Art thou waking?
      Lilith, I live!
      Closer my babe!

      Far o'er the dun wold,
      Baby, behold
'Mid the mist and the snow, fast, fast, and more fast—
In the teeth of the blast—flies Lilith at last.
      Pale Lilith flies!
      Nearer, my babe!

By Ganges still the Indian mother weaves
Above her babe her mat of plantain leaves,
And laughing, plaits. Or pausing, sweet and low
Her voice blends with the river's drowsy flow;
The while she fitful sings that old, old strain,
Forgetting that the love, the deathless pain
Of wandering Lilith lives and throbs again
When falls the tricksy Elf-babes' mocking cry
Faintly across her crooning lullaby—

Ah, happy babe, that here may sleep
    Where the blue river winds along,
And sweet the trysting bulbuls keep
    The night o'er-brimmed with pulsing song.

Not so, mine own, as legends tell,
    In lands remote, beyond the day,
The soulless babes of Lilith dwell,
    Or vanish 'mong the cold mists gray.

Or oft in elfin glee they ride
    O'er burning deserts blown adrift,
Or singing idly, idly glide
    Afar beyond Night's purple rift.

But thou, my babe, for thee shall grow
    The lilies, nodding by the stream;

For thee, the poppy's sleepy glow;
    For thee, the jonquil's pallid gleam.

My baby, sleep! Against the sky
    The pippul lifts its trembling crest.
O baby, hush each wailing cry,
    Close to the holy river's breast.

Not here shall come that pale wraith fair,
    Who, wandering once in Northern lands,
Bore o'er long reaches sere and bare
    The death-flower white, for baby hands.

Fear not, mine own, the Elf-babes shrill,
    Nor Lilith tall, with brow of snow.
They may not haunt thy slumbers still
    Where Ganges' sacred waters flow.

Where coral reefs gnaw with white cruel teeth
The yellow surf, and the torn billows seethe—
When shines the Southern Cross o'er placid isles,
The Afric mother sits, and singing, smiles,
Unheeding that a dead world's hidden pain
Beats wildly rhythmic through her pure refrain,
And lingers softly still an echoed sigh
Low in Earth's cradle-song—sweet lullaby.
A warning song of doom—a song of woe,
Of terror wild, she sings, down bending low,
The while bright gleams the Starry Cross above
Yet tells to her no tale of tender love
Of Him who lifteth after-time a cross
That healeth all the wide world's sin and loss.

Ah, linger no longer 'mong blooms of the mangoes,
    Nor pluck the bright shells by the low sighing sea,
Swift, swift, through the groves of the palms and acacias
    Comes Lilith, the childless one, seeking for thee.
She will bind thee so fast in her yellow-gold hair—
    Ah, hasten, my children, of Lilith beware!

Cold, cold are her cheeks as the spray of the wild sea,

Red, red are her lips as the pomegranate's bloom;
Cold, cold are the kisses the phantom will give thee,
　　　Ah, cruel her kisses, that smell of the tomb.
Hist, hist! 'tis the sorceress with yellow-gold hair—
　　　Oh! lullaby, baby—of Lilith beware.

She flies to the jungle, with false tales beguiling,
　　　Ah, hear'st thou her elfin babes scream overhead!
Close, close in her strong arms she bears my babe, smiling;
　　　She hath sucked the soft bloom from the lips of my dead.
Now far speeds the vampire, with yellow-gold hair—
　　　Oh! lullaby, baby—of Lilith beware!

Art frighted, my baby? Nay, then, thy mother
　　　Low singing enfolds thee all safe from the snare;
Afar flit the Elf-babes 'mid gray, misty shadows,
　　　Afar flees the temptress with yellow-gold hair.
Ah, heed not her songs in the still slumbrous air—
　　　Oh! lullaby, baby—of Lilith beware!

When hawthorn-trees sift thick their rifted snow,
The English mother o'er her babe sings low;
Where red the cross burns on the ivied fane,
Unwitting, pagan Lilith lives again—
And softer sings, nor feels the wailing pain
Still faintly surging through that low refrain;
Nor dreams she hears Love's early cradle cry
Slow echoing through Earth's song—sweet lullaby—
And in the shadow of that cross, her strain
Breathes sweetly; love, and hope, and ended pain.
Softlier while that small arm closely clings
 About her heart, that mother peaceful sings:

　　O babe, my babe, the light doth fade!
　　　　My baby, sleep, while I do keep
　　Close watch, where thou art lowly laid.
　　　　Sweet dreams shall steep thy slumber deep.
　　　　Ah, little feet, be still at last—
　　Rest all the night, for day is past;
　　One watches thee from yon blue sky,
　　One watching here sings lullaby,

>   Lullaby;
>   Sings lullaby.

Here on his bed the sunny head
>   Lies still; and soft the brown eyes close;
Sweet steals the breath, 'twixt lips as red,
>   As dewy fresh, as new-born rose.
>   O little lips, be hushed at last;
Fear naught, sweetheart, though day be past.
One looks adown from yon far sky,
One close beside, sings lullaby,
>   Lullaby;
>   Sings lullaby.

www.ingramcontent.com/pod-product-compliance
Lightning Source LLC
Chambersburg PA
CBHW042120100526
44587CB00025B/4130